THE TOILET BOOK

...INTERESTING FACTS NOT OLNY ABOUT POOPS

Tintoria

Feces, often referred to as poop, are the result of the body's digestion process, expelling waste that can't be absorbed by the body. This substance is vital for maintaining health by removing unwanted materials. The composition and appearance of feces can vary significantly, offering insights into an individual's diet, lifestyle, and overall health. Regular bowel movements are a sign of a healthy digestive system.

Urine is a liquid by-product of metabolism in humans and many animals. Primarily composed of water, it also contains an array of dissolved solids, including urea, chloride, sodium, potassium, creatinine, and other metabolic waste products. The kidneys filter these substances from the blood, making urine a crucial component in the body's process of removing toxins and maintaining a stable internal environment.

The modern flush toilet was invented in the 16th century by Sir John Harington, godson of Queen Elizabeth I. His design, called the Ajax, was a precursor to the toilets we use today. Harington's invention included a valve at the bottom of the bowl to retain water after flushing, a feature still central to today's designs.

Wombat feces are cube-shaped, a unique adaptation that prevents them from rolling away. This shape helps wombats mark their territory and communicate through scent. The cubic form is due to the elasticity of their intestines and how the feces dry in the final sections of the gut

In Japan, high-tech toilets, known as Washlets, are a staple in many households. These sophisticated devices offer features like bidet washing, seat warming, and even air drying, providing a luxurious and hygienic bathroom experience. The culture places a high value on cleanliness, and these toilets reflect that priority, blending technology with tradition in daily life.

Natural Process: Farting is a natural biological process, resulting from the digestion of food. As the stomach and intestines break down food, gases such as nitrogen, carbon dioxide, oxygen, methane, and hydrogen are produced and expelled through the rectum.

The color of urine can range from pale yellow to deep amber, depending on the concentration of urochrome, a pigment produced from the breakdown of hemoglobin. The color can also be influenced by hydration levels, diet, and certain medications, serving as a useful indicator of health and hydration status.

Composed primarily of water, feces also contain a mixture of undigested food residue, bacteria, and cells shed from the mucous membrane of the intestinal wall. The bacterial content is particularly significant, as it plays a crucial role in the digestive process and in maintaining gut health. The balance of these components can affect stool consistency and frequency.

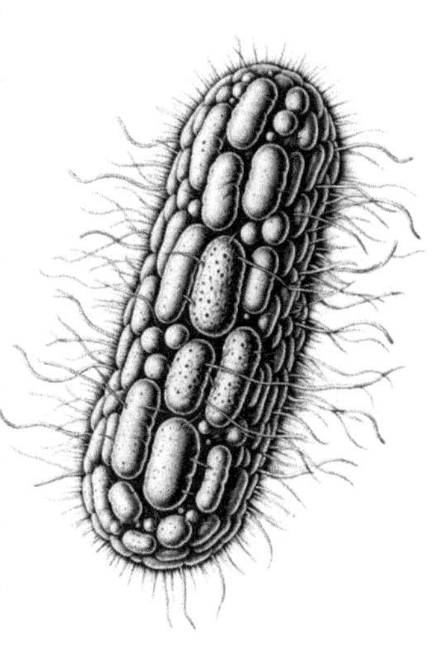

The word "toilet" comes from the French "toilette," which referred to the act of dressing and grooming. Over time, the term evolved to include the fixtures used in the process, including the washbasin and eventually the device we know today.

Hyenas use their feces as a communication tool, depositing them in communal spots known as latrines. These fecal deposits convey social status and territorial boundaries. The white color of hyena feces comes from the high concentration of calcium they ingest by consuming animal bones.

In many parts of India, the traditional practice of open defecation is being challenged by the government's "Clean India" campaign, which aims to build millions of toilets to improve public health and sanitation. This massive effort highlights the cuElephants produce up to 150 kilograms of feces per day, which plays a significant role in enriching the soil and spreading seeds. Many plant species depend on passing through an elephant's digestive tract to germinate, making elephants key players in their ecosystems.ltural shift towards prioritizing hygiene and the environment, acknowledging the importance of sanitary facilities for all.

Urine production can vary greatly, with a healthy adult producing about 1 to 2 liters per day. This output is influenced by factors such as fluid intake, activity level, environmental temperature, and the body's physiological state.

The characteristic odor of feces is due to microbial action in the intestines, where bacteria break down food materials, releasing gases and volatile compounds like indole, skatole, and sulfur-containing substances. These by-products are responsible for the strong and often unpleasant smell of bowel movements.

Elephants produce up to 150 kilograms of feces per day, which plays a significant role in enriching the soil and spreading seeds. Many plant species depend on passing through an elephant's digestive tract to germinate, making elephants key players in their ecosystems.

In rural areas of Indonesia, particularly in Java, traditional latrines, known as "jamban," are built over bodies of water. The waste directly enters the water, a practice now being addressed by public health initiatives aiming to introduce more sustainable and hygienic sanitation methods to prevent waterborne diseases and protect marine life.

Silent but Deadly: The notorious "silent but deadly" farts owe their stealth and potent smell to a high concentration of sulfur-containing gases, produced by the digestion of certain foods like broccoli, meat, and eggs.

Fecal consistency can vary from hard and pellet-like to loose and watery, reflecting the body's fluid balance and dietary intake. Consistency is an important indicator of digestive health, with deviations often signaling issues such as dehydration, dietary problems, or gastrointestinal disorders.

Guano, the accumulated excrement of seabirds and bats, is highly prized as a natural fertilizer due to its rich content of nitrogen, phosphorus, and potassium. The harvesting of guano has played a significant role in agriculture in certain parts of the world.

The process of urination, or micturition, involves a complex interplay of the nervous system, which coordinates the relaxation of the urinary sphincter and the contraction of the bladder muscles. This voluntary control allows individuals to decide when and where to urinate.

Birds excrete nitrogenous waste as uric acid instead of urea, resulting in the white, pasty portion of bird droppings. This adaptation helps conserve water, crucial for birds as they have high metabolic rates but limited access to water sources.

The average person spends about three years of their life on the toilet. Considering the frequency and necessity of its use, the toilet's design and functionality have a significant impact on daily comfort and sanitation.

Loud and Proud: The sound of a fart is produced by the vibrations of the rectum and the pressure of the gas being released. The volume and pitch can vary based on the tightness of the sphincter muscles and the amount of gas.

In Scandinavian countries, particularly Sweden, environmentally friendly dry toilets are popular in rural and wilderness areas. These toilets do not use water but instead compost human waste, turning it into a resource for gardening and agriculture. This practice highlights a cultural commitment to sustainability and respect for the natural environment.

Methane Producers: Not everyone produces methane in their farts. Only about one-third of the population has gut microbiomes that generate methane, which can make their gas flammable.

Feces, are composed of waste products that the body doesn't absorb during digestion. Their composition can vary based on diet and health but generally includes:

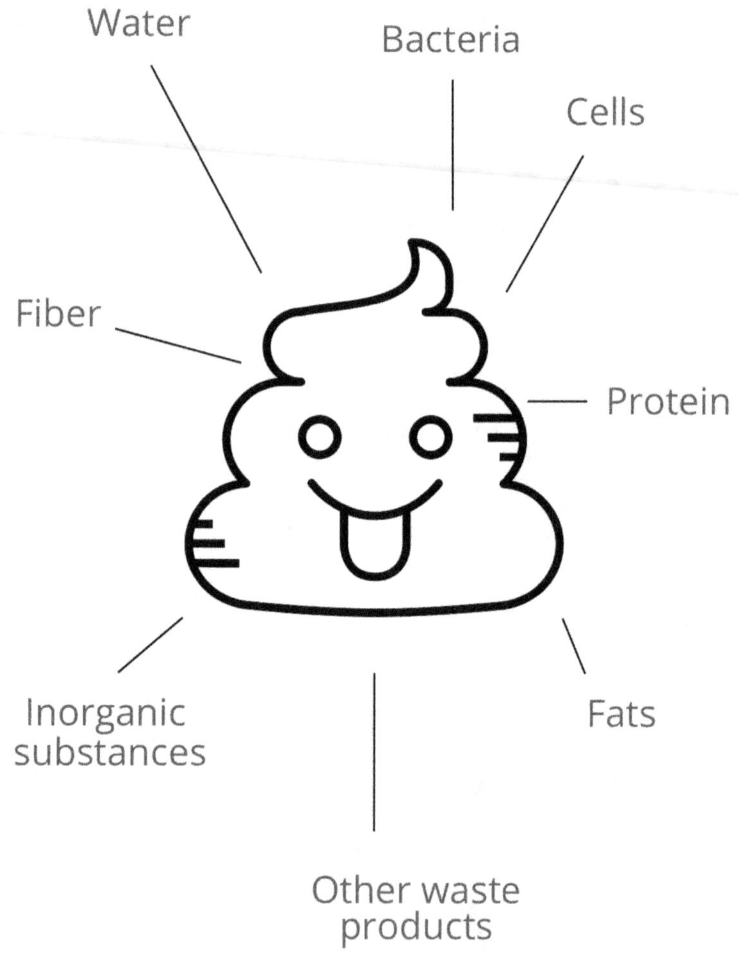

Urine has been used in diagnostic medicine for thousands of years. The presence of certain substances in urine can indicate a wide range of health conditions, from diabetes to kidney disease, making urinalysis a standard medical test.

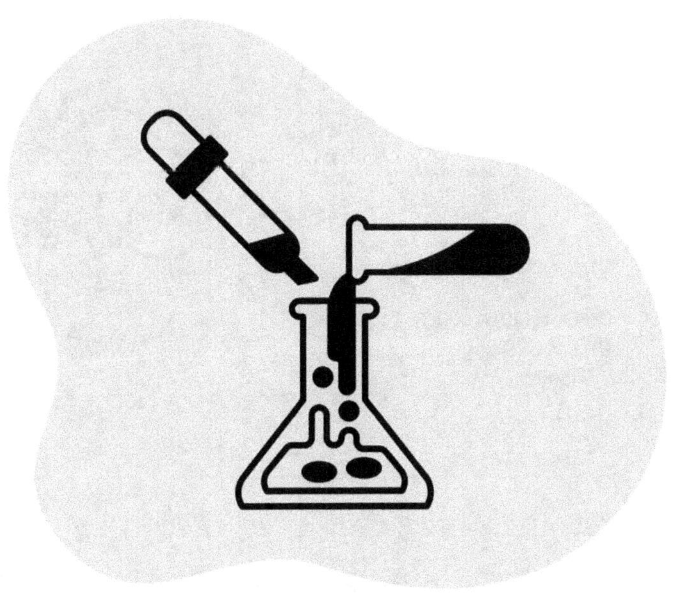

Coprophagia, the act of consuming feces, is observed in some animals as a way to digest food more thoroughly or obtain nutrients not absorbed during the first digestion. In humans, this behavior is rare and usually associated with certain mental health conditions or nutritional deficiencies.

Urophagia, the consumption of urine, is a practice observed in some cultures and alternative medicine circles, believed to have therapeutic benefits. However, there is little scientific evidence to support these claims, and consuming urine can introduce harmful substances back into the body.

Koala feces are small, pellet-like, and have a distinctive eucalyptus smell due to their diet of eucalyptus leaves. These pellets help researchers and conservationists track koala populations and health in the wild.

World Toilet Day is observed on November 19th each year, aiming to raise awareness about the global sanitation crisis and the importance of clean, accessible toilets for all. This day underscores the role of toilets in achieving public health, dignity, and well-being.

Speed of Sound: A fart exits the body at an impressive speed of about 10 feet per second, or nearly 7 miles per hour. This rapid expulsion is what sometimes leads to the humorous sounds associated with farting.

In the wild, animals use feces for various purposes, such as marking territory, deterring predators, or even as a component in building materials. The scent of feces can communicate vital information about an animal to others of the same species.

In ancient Rome, urine was highly valued for its ammonia content and was used for several purposes, including teeth whitening and laundering clothes. Collecting urine was a common practice, with public urinals emptying into vats that were then used by fullers (laundry workers).

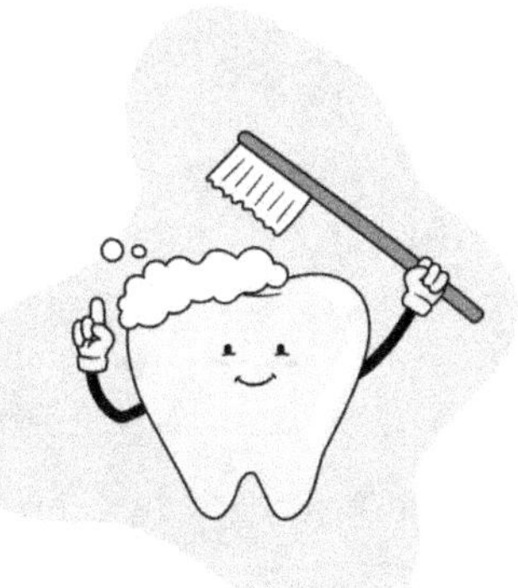

The International Space Station features a highly advanced toilet system designed to operate in zero gravity. It uses air flow instead of water to transport waste, which is then treated and recycled into drinking water, showcasing incredible advances in sustainability and resource management.

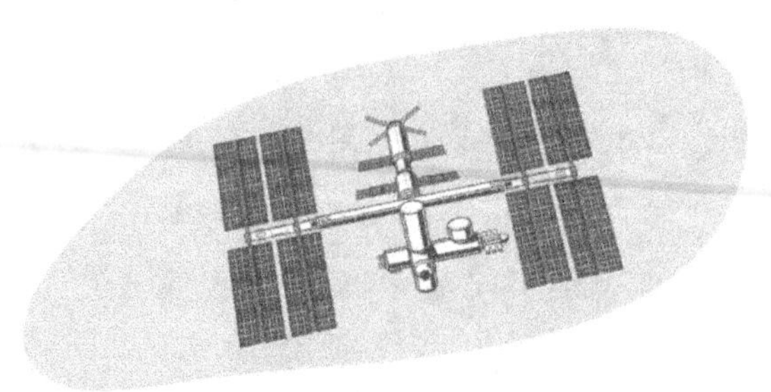

Termite feces, or frass, are used to construct mounds and tunnels. Termites mix their feces with saliva and soil, creating a strong, cement-like substance that is resistant to predators and environmental extremes.

In ancient Rome, communal latrines were a place for socialization and business, illustrating the social aspect of human sanitation practices. Romans would sit side by side with minimal privacy, discussing politics or the latest news, indicating how cultural norms around privacy and sanitation have evolved over time.

The scent of urine can change based on diet, hydration levels, and health conditions. For example, consuming asparagus can cause a distinctive and often unpleasant odor due to the breakdown of asparagusic acid.

In France, the bidet, although less common today, was once a staple in personal hygiene. This fixture, designed for washing the lower body, reflects the French emphasis on cleanliness and luxury. The cultural appreciation for the bidet underscores the diversity of hygiene practices around the world.

Average Daily Count: The average person farts around 14 to 23 times a day. This frequency is a normal part of the digestive process, helping to release excess gas produced during food breakdown.

The flushing toilet's popularity and development were significantly advanced by Thomas Crapper, a 19th-century English plumber and businessman. Though he did not invent the toilet, his improvements to the siphon mechanism and marketing savvy helped popularize it.

Certain animals use urine to mark their territory. The chemicals and pheromones in urine can convey information about the animal's identity, health status, and reproductive availability to others of the same species.

The first public pay toilets in England were installed at The Great Exhibition in 1851. For a penny, users received a clean seat, a towel, a comb, and a shoe shine, coining the phrase "spending a penny" to refer to using the toilet.

In rural Ethiopia, the "honey bucket" system is used in areas without plumbing. Families use a bucket for waste collection, which is then disposed of or composted. This practice highlights the challenges and solutions in sanitation faced by communities living in remote areas, demonstrating adaptability and resourcefulness.

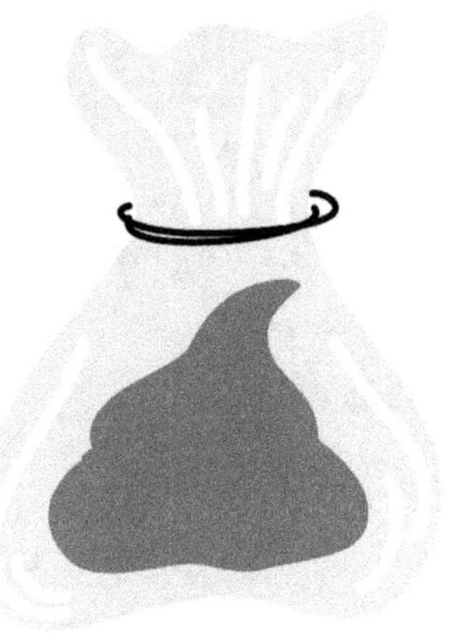

Sleep Farting: People fart in their sleep just as they do when awake. The body continues to digest food and expel gas, regardless of consciousness.

Urine can foam when it hits the toilet water, which is usually harmless and related to the urine's speed and the chemical reaction with water. However, persistent foaming can sometimes indicate excess protein in the urine, suggesting kidney issues.

In Mongolia, many nomadic families use portable tents as toilets, moving them as they relocate their camps. This mobility reflects the nomadic lifestyle, showing how sanitation practices are adapted to fit the cultural and environmental needs of people living in close harmony with the natural world.

Kopi Luwak, one of the world's most expensive coffees, is produced from coffee beans that have passed through the digestive system of the civet cat. The beans are believed to acquire a unique flavor from the enzymes present in the animal's stomach.

Fecal microbiota transplantation involves transferring stool from a healthy donor to a recipient's gastrointestinal tract to treat certain conditions, such as Clostridium difficile infection. This procedure can restore the recipient's gut flora balance and improve their digestive health.

Throughout history, urine has played a role in the production of gunpowder. Potassium nitrate, a key ingredient, can be extracted from urine-soaked soil, making urine a valuable resource in early munitions manufacture.

In ancient Rome, communal toilets were a common feature, highlighting the Romans' advanced approach to public sanitation. These facilities often included a shared sponge on a stick for cleaning, a testament to the communal nature of Roman life.

Diet Influence: The food we eat has a significant impact on our fart production. High-fiber foods increase gas, while certain carbohydrates that aren't fully digested in the stomach or small intestine lead to more fermentation in the gut.

Urine is a liquid waste product that is produced by the kidneys as they filter harmful substances from the blood. The composition of urine can vary based on a person's diet, hydration level, and overall health, but it typically includes the following components:

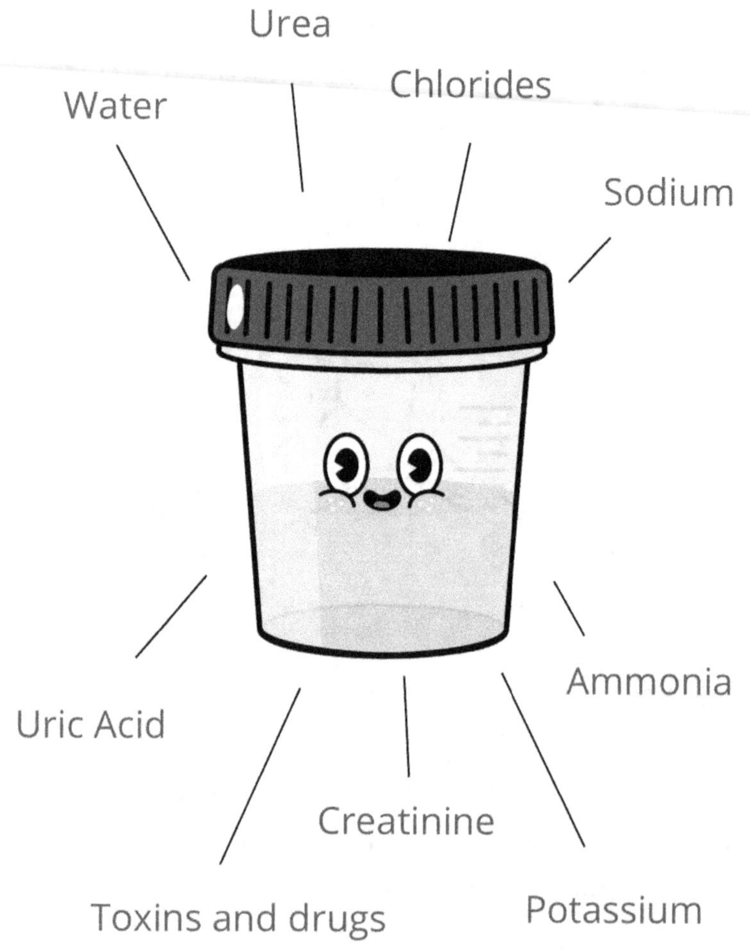

In medieval Europe, the disposal of human feces often involved simply throwing it out of windows onto the streets below, leading to unsanitary conditions that contributed to the spread of diseases like cholera and the plague.

Health Indicator: The characteristics of farts, such as frequency, smell, and volume, can sometimes indicate health issues. Excessive farting or particularly foul-smelling gas can be a sign of food intolerance or digestive problems.

Scatology, the study of feces, offers valuable insights into the diets, lifestyles, and health of both current populations and ancient civilizations. Analyzing fecal matter can reveal information about an individual's or community's nutritional habits, gastrointestinal health, and even the presence of parasites.

The **"Throne of Dagobert"** is an ornate folding chair believed to be the oldest surviving toilet, dating back to the 7th century. Originally belonging to King Dagobert of the Franks, it symbolizes the long history and cultural significance of toilets.

Rabbit feces are small, round pellets that are often reingested. This process, called coprophagy, allows rabbits to extract essential nutrients and vitamins from their food that were not absorbed during the first pass through the gut.

Underwater Farts: Farts can be more pungent when released underwater due to the increased surface area for the smell to dissolve into the water, making them seem stronger when bubbles reach the surface.

Feces can harbor harmful pathogens, including bacteria, viruses, and parasites, which can contaminate water sources and food supplies, leading to outbreaks of diseases such as cholera, typhoid, and hepatitis. Proper sanitation and hygiene practices are essential to prevent the spread of these diseases.

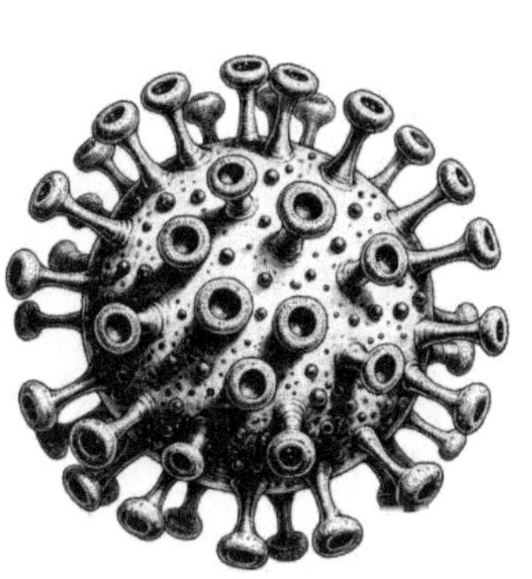

During the Victorian era, the design and decoration of toilets became a matter of fashion. Ornate patterns, wooden seats, and high-level cisterns with pull chains exemplified the era's aesthetic, blending functionality with style.

Penguin feces, or guano, can be seen from space. Researchers use satellite images to locate penguin colonies by spotting the dark stains of guano on the ice, aiding in the study of penguin populations and climate change impacts.

Biogas is a renewable energy source produced by the anaerobic digestion of organic materials, including human and animal feces. This process generates methane, which can be used for heating, cooking, and generating electricity, offering a sustainable alternative to fossil fuels.

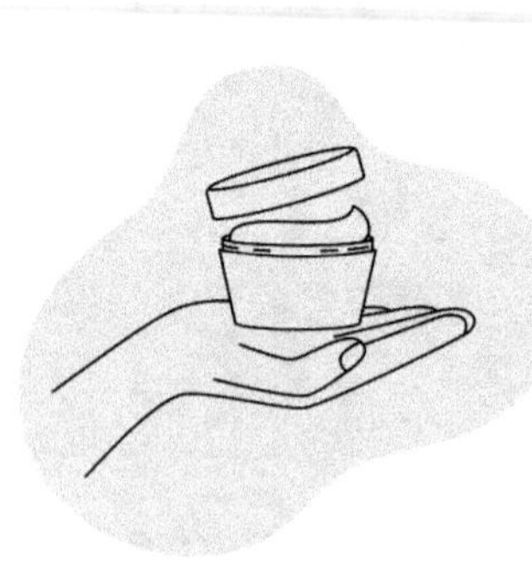

Feces can harbor harmful pathogens, including bacteria, viruses, and parasites, which can contaminate water sources and food supplies, leading to outbreaks of diseases such as cholera, typhoid, and hepatitis. Proper sanitation and hygiene practices are essential to prevent the spread of these diseases.

The Guggenheim Museum in New York once featured a fully functional gold toilet created by artist Maurizio Cattelan. Titled "America," the installation was both a work of art and a commentary on the excesses of modern society.

Historical Humor: Farting has been a source of humor and embarrassment throughout history. Famous figures like Benjamin Franklin penned essays on farting, highlighting its enduring presence in human culture.

Archaeological studies often include the analysis of fecal matter, or coprolites, to gain insights into the diet and health of ancient populations. These studies can reveal what people ate, how they cooked their food, and even which diseases they suffered from.

Urine's freezing point is lower than water's due to its solute content, a fact that has implications for survival in cold environments and the study of animal behavior in freezing temperatures.

Skunks use their feces as a defensive tool, leaving droppings near their dens as a warning to predators. The feces contain compounds that produce a strong odor, deterring potential threats.

Scientific Study: Farting is a subject of scientific study, particularly in the field of gastroenterology. Researchers explore how different foods affect gas production and how this can impact health.

Space missions must carefully manage human waste, including feces, to prevent contamination of the spacecraft environment. Astronauts use specially designed toilets that can operate in zero gravity, and the collected waste is often brought back to Earth for disposal.

The concept of dual-flush toilets, offering two flush options to conserve water, was introduced by Australian inventor Bruce Thompson in 1980. This innovation has since become a global standard in eco-friendly bathroom design.

Beavers use their feces to strengthen the waterproofing of their dams. The feces mix with mud and wood, creating a more solid and durable structure that helps maintain the beaver's aquatic habitat.

Prebiotics and Probiotics: Consuming prebiotics and probiotics can influence farting by altering the gut microbiome. These dietary supplements can help balance the digestive system and reduce gas production.

The practice of using human feces as fertilizer, known as "night soil," is still prevalent in some regions. While it can enrich soil with nutrients, it also poses health risks if not properly treated to kill pathogens.

In medieval castles, toilets known as "garderobes" were often built into the thickness of the walls, with chutes leading away from the living areas. These early toilets highlight the ingenuity of medieval architecture in incorporating sanitation.

Synthetic urine is produced for various uses, including calibrating urinalysis equipment, testing diapers, and as a novelty item. Its composition mimics that of real urine, without the health risks associated with handling biological waste.

Flammable Farts: The methane and hydrogen in farts make them flammable. This fact has been the basis of many a prank, though it's not recommended to try igniting farts due to the risk of injury.

The first urinalysis may have been conducted by Hippocrates, who suggested that the appearance, smell, and taste of urine could indicate disease. This practice laid the groundwork for modern diagnostic methods.

The Jemaa el-Fnaa square in Marrakech, Morocco, is home to a traditional Moroccan toilet facility that dates back hundreds of years, offering a glimpse into the enduring practices of public sanitation.

Capybara feces are an important nutrient source for aquatic ecosystems. As the largest rodent species, their droppings disperse seeds and contribute to the nutrient cycle in wetland environments.

Flatulence, commonly referred to as a fart, is the release of gas from the digestive system through the anus. The composition of flatulence varies among individuals based on diet, the balance of gut microbiota, and overall health. However, it generally consists of a mixture of gases, which include:

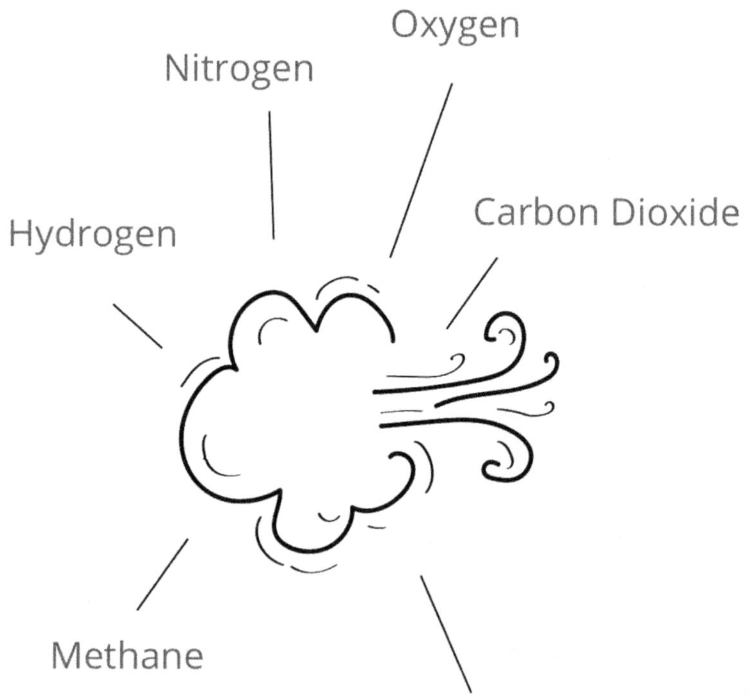

Record-Breaking: There are world records for just about everything, including farting. The longest recorded fart lasted 2 minutes and 42 seconds, a testament to the body's capacity for gas production.

Animal feces are used in some traditional medicines across various cultures, believed to cure ailments ranging from skin conditions to digestive disorders. This practice reflects the diverse ways in which human societies utilize natural resources for health purposes.

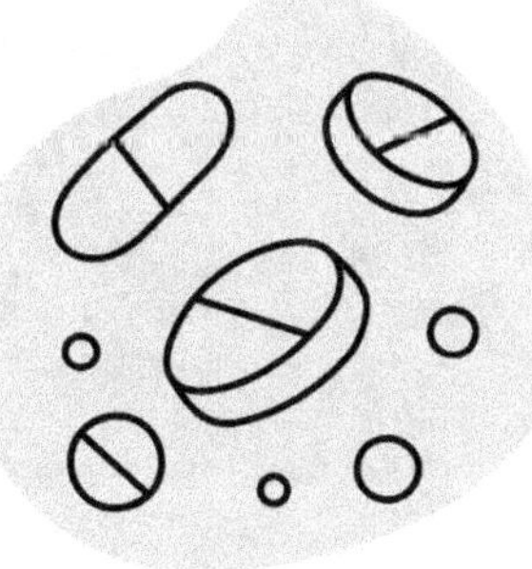

The shape and size of feces can be indicators of gastrointestinal health, with deviations from the norm potentially signaling issues such as blockages, IBS, or other conditions. Monitoring these aspects can help in early detection and management of health issues.

In zero-gravity environments, astronauts use specially designed toilets that use air flow to control the direction of urine, preventing it from floating away. This innovation is crucial for long-duration space missions, ensuring hygiene and comfort for the crew.

In South Korea, the Mr. Toilet House, a museum dedicated to the history and cultural significance of toilets, was founded by Sim Jae-duck, affectionately known as "Mr. Toilet." The museum, shaped like a toilet bowl, underscores the importance of sanitation and toilet innovation.

The Malayan civet uses its feces to mark its territory, leaving droppings in strategic locations. This not only communicates the civet's presence but also helps to deter intruders and establish mating rights within their habitat.

Some fish species produce fecal casts, encapsulating their waste in mucous shells. This process helps maintain water quality and can play a role in the dispersal of seeds consumed by the fish, contributing to the health of aquatic ecosystems.

Relief and Embarrassment:
While releasing a fart can provide physical relief, it often comes with social embarrassment. This duality reflects the natural human conflict between bodily needs and societal norms.

Toilet paper was first introduced in China in the 6th century, but it wasn't until the late 19th century that it became widely available in the West. Today, the choice of toilet paper (soft, strong, scented) reflects personal preference and cultural differences in hygiene.

Dung beetles play a critical ecological role by breaking down animal feces, thereby recycling nutrients back into the soil and reducing the spread of parasites and diseases. Their activity supports soil health and agricultural productivity.

Farting in Space: Astronauts fart in space just as they do on Earth. However, without gravity to separate gas from liquid and solid in the stomach, farting can be a more complex and uncomfortable process in space.

The practice of using toilets extends beyond humans; some cat owners train their pets to use the toilet, a testament to the adaptability of both species and the universal need for sanitary waste disposal.

Conservationists use fecal analysis to monitor the health and diet of endangered species without needing to capture or disturb the animals. This non-invasive method allows for the collection of valuable data on species' health and ecological interactions.

In Sweden, urine-diverting toilets are gaining popularity as a means to recycle nutrients. These toilets separate urine from feces, facilitating the recycling of urine as a fertilizer and reducing the environmental impact of waste.

Fart Jokes: Fart jokes are among the oldest forms of humor, dating back to ancient civilizations. This enduring humor suggests a universal human reaction to the absurdity and embarrassment of farting.

In rural communities, cow dung is collected, dried, and used as a fuel source for cooking and heating. This practice not only provides a renewable energy source but also helps in managing agricultural waste.

The flush toilet's water consumption has been a subject of environmental concern, leading to the development of low-flow and waterless toilets, emphasizing the balance between sanitation and sustainability.

Farting and Dieting: Changes in diet, especially those involving increased fiber intake, can lead to temporary increases in farting as the body adjusts to the new foods.

Researchers are exploring the use of human feces as a material for making sustainable bricks. This innovative approach aims to address sanitation issues while providing a low-cost building material.

The squat toilet, common in many Asian and Middle Eastern countries, is designed for users to squat rather than sit. This position is considered by many to be more natural and can help prevent bowel health issues. The design reflects a blend of cultural tradition and health-conscious practices, emphasizing the variety in human sanitation habits.

The tradition of "toilet reading" highlights the toilet's role as a private retreat for contemplation and leisure, with literature ranging from magazines to smartphones enriching the experience.

In 1775, Alexander Cumming received the first patent for a flush toilet. His design included an S-shaped pipe below the bowl that used water to create a seal preventing sewer gases from entering buildings, an innovation still in use.

The Netherlands is known for having some of the cleanest public toilets in the world, reflecting the Dutch value of cleanliness and public responsibility. Many of these facilities are equipped with self-cleaning seats, ensuring a hygienic experience for every user and showcasing the country's innovative approach to public sanitation.

Gender Differences: While studies suggest that men and women fart approximately the same amount, societal expectations often make it more taboo for women to acknowledge or joke about it.

Speed of Sound: A fart exits the body at an impressive speed of about 10 feet per second, or nearly 7 miles per hour. This rapid expulsion is what sometimes leads to the humorous sounds associated with farting.

In medieval Europe, urine was used as a mordant in dyeing cloth, helping to fix dyes to the fabric. This practice highlights the chemical properties of urine and its utility in various trades.

In ancient times, toilets and sanitation systems were a sign of wealth and civilization, with elaborate sewage systems in places like Mohenjo-Daro (Indus Valley Civilization) and Crete (Minoan Civilization) demonstrating advanced engineering and public health awareness.

Holding It In: While it might seem polite to hold in a fart, doing so can lead to discomfort and even pain. The gas can be reabsorbed into the circulation and expelled through the breath.

Odor Intensity: The intensity of a fart's odor can be influenced by several factors, including the amount of sulfur in the diet. Meats, garlic, and certain vegetables can lead to more potent smells.

The future of toilets involves advancements in biotechnology, including toilets that can monitor health metrics such as glucose levels, potential infections, and dietary insights, making the toilet an integral part of home health care.

Sloths descend from their arboreal habitats once a week to defecate at the base of trees, a risky move that makes them vulnerable to predators. This behavior is thought to help fertilize the soil and promote the growth of beneficial fungi.

Animal Farters: Humans aren't the only creatures that fart. Many animals, including dogs, cats, and even fish, release gas as part of their digestive process.

The use of camel dung as fuel is a traditional practice in many desert regions. It's dried and burned for cooking and heating, offering an efficient and readily available energy source in arid environments.

Farting Etiquette: Many societies have unwritten rules or etiquette about farting, such as excusing oneself from a room or blaming it on the nearest pet. These social norms help manage the natural, yet often stigmatized, act of farting.

Diabetics' urine was historically used to diagnose the disease, as it would attract ants due to its high sugar content. This method was one of the earliest forms of diabetes detection before modern testing techniques.

Camel urine has been consumed in some Middle Eastern cultures for centuries, believed to have medicinal properties. However, health authorities caution against this practice due to the risk of disease transmission.

Cultural Perceptions: Attitudes towards farting vary widely across cultures, with some viewing it as a humorous and natural bodily function, while others see it as rude and inappropriate in public settings.

The petrified feces of ancient animals, known as coprolites, provide valuable insights into the diets and ecosystems of extinct species. Coprolites have been found containing undigested food particles, parasites, and even fragments of other animals.

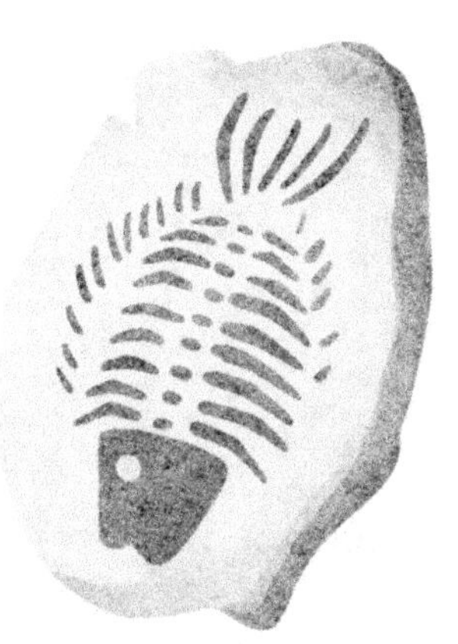

Singapore's Changi Airport boasts some of the world's most luxurious toilets, complete with orchids, full-length doors for privacy, and even a rooftop garden, redefining expectations for public restroom facilities.

Gorillas have been observed using their feces as a tool, manipulating it to communicate displeasure or aggression. This behavior underscores the complexity of gorilla social interactions and communication methods.

Fart Filtering Products: There are products on the market designed to filter or disguise the smell of farts, including underwear liners and pads. These items use activated carbon to neutralize odors, making social situations a bit less daunting.

The concept of portable toilets, crucial for outdoor events and construction sites, was developed in the 1940s in California, providing a practical solution to the need for temporary sanitation facilities.

9 7 9 8 8 8 4 0 2 0 7 7 1